KEEPING UP WITH YOU

A Practical Guide to Budgeting, Debt, Investing, Retirement, and Financial Dignity

Vincent C. Perry, CFP®

Printed in the United States of America
ISBN: 979-8-234-18254-8

This book is provided for educational and informational purposes only. It is not intended as individualized financial, investment, tax, legal, or insurance advice, and it does not create an advisory relationship.

Financial circumstances vary. Readers should consult appropriately qualified professionals before making decisions involving investments, retirement accounts, taxes, insurance, annuities, education funding, credit, or other financial matters.

Examples and illustrations are hypothetical unless otherwise stated. Past performance and investment results are not guaranteed. Investment values may fluctuate, and investors may experience gains or losses.

CFP® is a certification mark owned by Certified Financial Planner Board of Standards, Inc. (CFP Board). Use of the CFP® mark indicates that the certificant has met CFP Board's certification requirements.

Dedication

To everyone seeking financial clarity, confidence, and dignity.
May this book help you build a life aligned with your values and goals.

If this book resonates with you, there's a next step. Visit:
www.VincentCPerry.com
to access your free financial clarity tools and learn more about available planning resources.

Table of Contents

Introduction1

Chapter 1 — Building the Wealth Mindset: Habits and Behavior5

Chapter 2 — Budgeting & Spending Plans: From Awareness to Action15

Chapter 3 — Building a Cash Reserve: Your Financial Safety Net25

Chapter 4 — Managing Debt & Credit: Taking Back Control37

Chapter 5 — Retirement Planning: Building Future Income with Intention47

Chapter 6 — Education Planning: Preparing for the Future with Purpose57

Chapter 7 — Protecting Assets & Managing Risk: Securing What You've Built65

Chapter 8 — Take Action: Your Financial Transformation Starts Now75

References85

About the Author87

Introduction

Let me ask you something...

Have you ever felt like you should be further along financially than you are right now?

Like you're working hard, earning more than you used to—yet somehow it still doesn't feel like enough?

Maybe you've looked around—at friends, coworkers, or even strangers online—and wondered:

"How are they doing it?"

"What am I missing?"

If so, you're not alone. In fact, you're exactly where many people find themselves—caught in the quiet tension between what life looks like and what it actually costs to live it.

In my first book, *Keeping Up With the Joneses? They're Broke Too!* we pulled back the curtain on that illusion. We explored how comparison, pressure, and perception can influence our financial decisions, often leading us to spend money we don't need to create a life that doesn't truly serve us. We uncovered a powerful truth: what looks like success from the outside is often built on fragile financial ground. But awareness is only the beginning.

This book—*Keeping Up with YOU*—is about what comes next.

This isn't about keeping up with anyone else.

It's about finally aligning your money with your life.

Your goals.

Your priorities.

Your version of success.

Because real financial progress doesn't happen when you try to match someone else's lifestyle, it happens when you take control of your own.

Inside these pages, you'll learn how to:

Take control of your cash flow instead of wondering where your money went

Build a financial plan that actually works in real life

Break the habits that quietly hold you back

Replace pressure and confusion with clarity and confidence!

Make decisions that move you forward—not just make you feel better in the moment

This is not a theory book.

It's a practical roadmap.

You'll see real-life examples—people who struggled, adjusted, and ultimately transformed their financial lives not because they earned more, but because they thought differently and acted intentionally. You'll also gain simple tools you can apply immediately, no matter where you're starting.

Because here's the truth:

Financial success is not about perfection.

It's about direction.

It's not about how much you make.

It's about what you keep, how you use it, and whether your money is working for you instead of against you.

And most importantly, it's about finally stepping off the comparison treadmill and building a life that feels good to live.

This book is about you.

Where you are right now.

Where you want to go.

And how to close the gap—one intentional decision at a time.

Because this journey isn't about keeping up with anyone else. It's about finally learning how to keep up with YOU. Let's get started.

Chapter 1 — Building the Wealth Mindset: Habits and Behavior

What Does Wealth Really Mean?

When you hear the word wealth, what comes to mind?
For many people, it's:
Money
Investments
Cars
Square footage

But true wealth reaches far beyond what can be measured on a balance sheet.

Wealth can be:
Peace of mind
Flexibility
Freedom
Control
The ability to make decisions without fear

The ability to live intentionally—rather than reactively.

Because before we can build wealth in our accounts...
We must first build wealth in our minds.

Redefining Success

This chapter challenges the traditional definition of success and invites you to redefine it—on your terms.

Not based on comparison.
Not based on pressure.
Not based on appearance.

But based on:
Clarity
Purpose
Disciplined action

As discussed in Keeping Up With the Joneses? many of our financial decisions are shaped by who we compare ourselves to—whether we realize it or not.

Sometimes the comparison is intentional.
Often, it's unconscious.

Social media.
Peers.
Our neighborhoods.
Even our workplaces.

All of these create standards of "success" that may not be financially healthy—or even realistic.

Without realizing it, we begin adjusting our behavior to match expectations that were never ours to begin with.

The Cost of "Looking Successful"

If the goal is simply to look successful, we end up spending money on things that create the illusion of progress—not the reality of it.
But real wealth is not about appearance.
It's about:
Control over your choices
Margin in your budget
Time to focus on what matters
Stability to weather storms
Peace knowing you're prepared

When success is defined by values instead of visuals, your spending naturally shifts.

You stop trying to impress others...
And start building a life that supports you.

Wealth happens when your money aligns with your purpose—not your pressure.

Case Study — Jane: A Familiar Story

Let's bring this to life.

Meet Jane.

(Not an actual client—but someone whose story represents many real people.)

Jane is a 31-year-old project manager living in a suburban neighborhood. She earns a solid income—more than she ever imagined when she started her career.

Yet somehow...

She always feels broke.

And if you remember from Keeping Up With the Joneses? "broke" isn't about income.

It's about mindset. It's about habits.

The Cycle Jane Didn't See

Every month, Jane faced a new financial "surprise":

A higher utility bill

A weekend outing that cost more than expected

Another online purchase she didn't remember making

Then one evening, scrolling through social media, it happened again.

A coworker posted pictures from a luxury trip to Greece. A friend showed off a brand-new car—the same model Jane once wanted.

Almost instantly, she felt it:

Frustration.

Pressure.

Confusion.

"I work just as hard. Why am I not there yet?"

The Turning Point

That night, Jane opened three tabs:
Flights
A car dealership
A credit card offer
She didn't need any of it.
But she felt behind.

And she was ready to spend money she didn't have to catch up with people who weren't thinking about her at all.
The next morning, reality hit.
Her bank balance said otherwise.

The Realization

Jane finally saw it clearly:
She wasn't competing with them.
She was competing with her own habits.

Why Habits Matter More Than Strategy

Even the best financial strategies fall apart without the right habits.
One of Jane's friends introduced her to a simple tool:

The 72-Hour Purchase Pause

Instead of buying impulsively, Jane wrote down "urgent wants" and waited three days.
Something interesting happened.
The car didn't feel necessary
The vacation felt like escapism
The credit card felt like a trap

Why It Works

The brain is wired for impulse.
Retailers know this. That's why you see:

"Limited time only!"
"Only a few left!"
"Sale ends tonight!"
The pause interrupts that cycle.
It shifts decision-making from emotional... to logical.

Questions That Change Everything

During those 72 hours, Jane began asking:
Will this move me closer to or farther from my goals?
Do I want this—or the feeling it gives me?
Is there a better alternative?
Would future me be proud of this decision?
Most of the time, the desire faded.
What remained... was clarity.

Case Study — Jane: Transformation

Jane didn't suddenly earn more money.
She changed how she thought about money.
Her behaviors shifted.
Over time, those small changes led to big results:
More savings
Less stress
Greater control
She learned a powerful truth:

Wealth starts in the mind—long before it shows up in your bank account.

Case Study — Bill & Mary: A Different Path

Now, meet Bill and Mary.
They've been married for over 40 years.

They still live in the same modest home they purchased decades ago.

It's not updated.
It's not flashy.
But it's paid off.
And more importantly—it reflects something rare:
Contentment.

Their Mindset

Every year, they ask three simple questions:
What matters to us this year?
What can we afford?
What can we live without?
They're not immune to comparison.
They simply don't give it power.

Their Habits

1. Intentional Spending
They spend deeply on what matters—not broadly on everything.
2. Save First
Saving isn't optional. It happens automatically.
3. The Pause Rule
They wait before making purchases.
Their decisions reflect values—not emotions.

A Moment That Says Everything

Friends of Bill and Mary once showed them a luxury SUV:
"You should get one. You've earned it."
Their response?
"It's nice... but it wouldn't make us any happier."
That's it.

No pressure.
No comparison.
No second-guessing.
Peace over prestige.

The Result

Today, Bill and Mary:
Have no debt
Have strong retirement savings
Live comfortably
Feel in control

They didn't build wealth through income.
They built it through clarity and consistency.
They built a life they didn't need to escape from.

The Wealth Mindset

A wealth mindset is not about restriction.
It's about intention.
It's built on four pillars:

1. Awareness

Understand:
Your habits
Your triggers
Your patterns

You cannot change what you don't examine.

2. Intention

Money flows toward what you prioritize.

If you don't define those priorities, something else will:
Advertising
Social pressure
Convenience

3. Discipline

Discipline isn't punishment.
It's consistency with purpose.

4. Patience

Wealth builds slowly.
Quietly.
Predictably.
Most people don't fail due to income.
They fail due to impatience.

The Power of "Enough"

One of the most powerful concepts in wealth building is... enough.
Enough doesn't limit your life.
It defines your life.
When you understand what "enough" looks like:
You stop chasing unnecessary upgrades
You stop comparing your life
You stop spending without purpose

Enough is clarity.
Enough is control.
Enough is wealth.

Apply It This Week

Start small:

Identify your comparison triggers
Define your "Enough Statement"
Use the 72-hour rule once

Track one habit

Celebrate small wins
Because progress builds confidence.
And confidence builds momentum.

Closing Thought

Wealth isn't something you find.
It's something you build—choice by choice.
You don't need to match anyone else's lifestyle.

You only need to build one that aligns with your values. Everything else in this book starts here.

Now that you understand how your mindset shapes your financial decisions, the next step is learning where your money is going—and how to take control of it.

Chapter 2 — Budgeting & Spending Plans: From Awareness to Action

When I meet with clients like Jane, or Bill and Mary, one principle always comes first:

No matter your financial goal, buying a home, saving for education, or planning for retirement—you must understand where you stand today.

Because before you can move forward...

You need a clear picture of your starting point.

Step One: Define What You're Working Toward

Start by getting clear on your goals.

Ask yourself:

What do I want to achieve financially?

What matters most to me right now?

What will matter five, ten, or twenty years from now?

Write your goals down.

Break them into:

Short-term

Mid-term

Long-term

Then prioritize them.

Because your money will always flow toward something —

The goal is to make sure it flows toward what matters most to you.

Step Two: Know Your Net Worth

Your net worth is your financial snapshot:
Assets – Liabilities = Net Worth
Track it over time.
Not to judge yourself—but to measure progress.
Because progress—no matter how small—builds momentum.

Case Study — Marc: He Didn't Think He Was Behind

Marc came into my office confident.

He earned over $120,000 a year.
Drove a nice car.
Lived in a great neighborhood.
By all outward appearances—he was doing well.
When I asked him about his net worth, he paused.
"I've never really calculated it," he said.
So, we did it together.

After listing everything out—his home, retirement account, car—and then subtracting:
Credit card balances
Student loans
Car loan
Mortgage
The number surprised him.
Not devastating...
But not what he expected either.
He leaned back and said:
"I thought I was ahead... but I've just been busy."
That moment mattered.
Because for the first time, Marc wasn't guessing.
He had clarity.
And clarity creates change.

Step Three: Understand Your Debt-to-Income Ratio

Your debt-to-income ratio (DTI) tells you how much of your income is going toward debt.
The lower it is:
The more flexibility you have
The less stress you feel
The easier it is to build wealth

This isn't just a bank number.
It's a lifestyle indicator.
Now let's talk about the most misunderstood tool...

The Budget

When you hear the word budget, what comes to mind?
For many people:
Restriction
Stress
Failure
But here's the truth:
A budget is not a punishment.
A budget is a plan.
And a plan is freedom.

Why Most Budgets Fail

Budgets don't fail because people lack discipline.
They fail because they don't reflect real life.

Case Study — Sarah: The Perfect Budget That Never Worked

Sarah did everything "right."
She created a spreadsheet.
Categorized every expense.
Set strict limits.

Her grocery budget? $200.
Dining out? $50.
On paper—it looked perfect.
In reality?
She was spending:
$450 on groceries
$300 eating out
By the end of every month, she quit tracking.
Why?
Because her budget didn't match her life.
During one meeting, I asked her:
"Sarah... is your goal to have a perfect budget—or a working budget?"
She smiled.

"Working," she said.
So, we adjusted it.
Not to what it should be.
But to what it actually was.
That's when things changed.

Three Rules for a Budget That Works

1. It Must Be Realistic
Truth beats aspiration.
2. It Must Be Simple
Complex systems fail quickly.
3. It Must Be Flexible
Life changes—your budget should too.

Where Awareness Begins

Most people think they know where their money goes...
Until they track it.

Case Study — Dan: The $800 Surprise

Dan swore he didn't spend much on food.
"I cook at home most of the time," he said.
So, I asked him to track his spending for 30 days.
At our next meeting, we went line by line.
Coffee here.
Lunch there.
A quick dinner on the way home.
Total?
$823.
He laughed—not because it was funny—
But because he had no idea.
"I thought it was maybe $200," he said.
That's the power of awareness.
Not judgment.
Just truth.

Your First Assignment

Track every dollar you spend for 30 days.
This is your financial X-ray.
You don't need to fix anything yet.
Just observe.

The Best Budget?

The one you will actually use.
Not the most advanced.
Not the most detailed.
The most consistent.

The Power of Automation

Automation removes friction.
It turns intention into action.
Automate:

Savings
Retirement
Bills
Debt
Because what's automatic...
Actually gets done.

Monthly Money Meetings (with yourself, or a loved one)

15 minutes.
Once a month.
Review:
What you planned
What you spent
What needs adjusting
Simple habits create powerful results.

The Two Decisions That Shape Everything

1. Housing
Target: 25–30% of income
2. Transportation
Target: Under 10% of income

Case Study — James & Renee: The House That Looked Right—but Felt Tight

James and Renee bought their "dream home."
Beautiful neighborhood.
Plenty of space.
Everything they wanted.
But within six months...
Things felt different.
They started saying:
"We can't do that right now"

"Let's put that off"
"We'll save later"
Their housing cost?
Nearly 42% of their income.
They hadn't made a bad decision—
They had made a *stretch* decision.
And now the rest of their life was adjusting to it.
During one session, Renee said something powerful:
"We don't feel rich... even though this house looks like we should."
That's the tradeoff many people don't see.

The Hidden Cost of "Just a Little More"

The same is true with cars.
"Just $200 more a month" feels small.
But over time?
That decision compounds.
Less savings.
Less flexibility.
More pressure.

The Big Picture

Housing + Transportation = 40%–55% of spending.
Get these right—and everything else becomes easier.

Final Thought: Your Budget Is a Tool—Not a Judge

You are not "bad" with money.
You are learning.
Remember
Perfection is not the goal.
Progress is the goal.
Overspending is feedback—not failure.

Closing Thought

A budget doesn't limit your life.
It gives you control over it.

Financial freedom doesn't come from earning more... It comes from using what you have—intentionally.

Once you understand your money, the next step is protecting it—so progress doesn't disappear the moment life becomes unpredictable.

Chapter 3 — Building a Cash Reserve: Your Financial Safety Net

Let's start with a simple, but important question:

What would you do if an unexpected expense hit tomorrow?

A car repair.

A medical bill.

A job interruption.

Would you feel prepared... or pressured?

A Reality Check

The data tells a powerful story.

63% of U.S. adults say they could cover a $400 emergency using cash, savings, or a credit card paid off immediately [1]

The remaining:

15% would carry credit card debt

10% would borrow from others

7% would sell something

13% couldn't cover it at all [1]

It gets even more concerning:

Only 47% of Americans could handle a $1,000 emergency without taking on debt [2]

Only 55% have at least three months of savings

Take a moment and think about that.

This is happening in one of the wealthiest countries in the world.

What Is a Cash Reserve?

A cash reserve (or emergency fund) is simply:
Money set aside for the unexpected.
It's not for vacations.
It's not for shopping.
It's for:
Job loss
Medical expenses
Home or auto repairs

Instead of relying on credit cards or loans, your cash reserve gives you options—and control.

Case Study — Jane: From Awareness to Stability

By the time Jane reached this point, she had already made some important changes.

In Chapter 1, she realized her habits—not her income—were driving her financial stress.

In Chapter 2, she built her first working budget.
Not perfect—but honest.
For the first time, she knew:
What was coming in
What was going out
Where the gaps were
But there was still a problem.
Even with a budget...
One unexpected expense could undo everything.

The Moment That Changed Her Thinking

It happened on a Tuesday morning.

Jane was heading to work when her car made a strange noise.

By the time she pulled into the mechanic's shop, she already felt it—that familiar tension.

An hour later, she got the call.

"Brake system issue. It's going to be about $1,400."

Her mind immediately started racing:

Do I put this on a credit card?

Can I delay it?

Do I have any other options?

She had just started getting control of her finances...

And now this.

What She Did Next

Jane used her credit card.

Not because she wanted to... but because she had to.

That night, sitting at her kitchen table, she looked at her budget.

For the first time, she saw something clearly:

Budgeting helped her plan.

But it didn't protect her.

Why This Matters

Without a cash reserve, every unexpected expense becomes a financial disruption.

Progress gets paused.

Debt increases

Stress rises

A cash reserve doesn't just protect your money.

It protects your peace of mind.

Case Study — Jane: New Priority

That experience changed her focus.

Before, she wanted to:
Spend less
Stay on budget

Now?
She wanted something different.
She wanted stability.
She told herself:
"I never want to feel that pressure again over something I can plan for."

That's when building a cash reserve became her top priority.

Case Study — Jack: The $2,000 Breakdown

Jack had just started making real financial progress.

He was budgeting.
Paying down debt.
Doing everything right.
Then his car broke down.
Cost: $2,000.
Without savings, he had two options:
Put it on a credit card

Delay the repair—and risk losing his transportation to work.

He chose the credit card.
That one decision erased months of progress.
Not because he was irresponsible...
But because he was unprepared.

Six months later, Jack had built a small emergency fund.
When another issue came up, he paid cash.
No stress.
No setback.
Just a solution.

That's the difference a cash reserve makes.

How Much Should You Have?

A common guideline is:
3–6 months of essential expenses.
This includes:
Housing
Transportation
Utilities
Groceries
Insurance
Healthcare
But the "right" amount depends on your situation.

Case Study — Jane: Starts Small

When Jane heard "3–6 months of expenses," her first reaction was:
"There's no way I can do that right now."
And that's where many people stop.
But instead of quitting, she reframed the goal.
Not 6 months.
Not even 3 months.
She started with $500.
Then:
$1,000
Then one month of expenses
She focused on progress—not perfection.

General Guidelines

Two-Income Households

You may be able to stay on the lower end of the range.

Single-Income Households

Consider leaning toward six months (or more).

Variable Income (commission, business owners)

A larger buffer helps manage income swings.

High-Income or Specialized Careers

A longer job search may require more savings.

Retirees

Cash reserves may need to cover 12–24 months of expenses in some cases.

Life Adjustments Matter

Certain situations may require more savings:
Older homes (higher repair risk)
High-deductible insurance plans
Long-distance family responsibilities
The goal is simple:

Build a reserve that matches your reality—not someone else's.

Where Should You Keep It?

Your emergency fund should be:
Accessible
Safe
Earning some return

You outlined a strong three-tier approach:

Tier 1: Immediate Access

Checking

High-yield savings
Cash management accounts
This is for urgent needs.

Tier 2: Short-Term Access (1–3 Months)

Money market funds
Investment certificates
This adds yield while maintaining access.

Tier 3: Medium-Term Access (3–12 Months)

Treasury bills
CDs
Ultra-short-term bond options
This helps your money work harder without sacrificing stability.

Case Study — Jane: Builds Her First Safety Net

Three months later, Jane checked her savings:
$2,300.
It wasn't a full emergency fund.
But it was enough to change how she felt.
She no longer felt:
Fragile
Reactive
One step behind
She felt… *prepared.*

Do You Need Alternatives?

In some cases, people consider backup options like:
Home equity lines of credit (HELOCs)
Securities-based lending
These can provide access to funds in emergencies.
But remember:

These are not substitutes for savings.
They are borrowed money—not **owned** money.

Case Study — Monica: Credit vs. Cash

Monica had access to a HELOC.
She felt confident.
"Worst case—I'll use that."
Then an emergency hit.
She used the credit line without hesitation.
But afterward?
She had:
Monthly payments
Interest costs
Added financial pressure

Later, she built a six-month emergency fund.
Same type of emergency... different outcome.

This time?
No debt.
No stress.
No disruption.

That's the difference between accessing money and owning money.

How Do You Build It?

If you don't yet have 3–6 months saved, don't panic.
Start small.

Case Study — Jane: What She Actually Did

Jane didn't build her emergency fund overnight.
She built it through simple, repeatable actions:

She automated $100 per paycheck into savings
She paused impulse purchases using the 72-hour rule
She redirected her tax refund instead of spending it
She reduced one subscription and saved the difference
Nothing dramatic.
Just consistent.
Month by month, her account started to grow.
At first, it didn't feel like much.
But something started to change.

Use a Systematic Approach

Treat your savings like a bill.
Not an afterthought.
Pay yourself first.
That means:
Save automatically
Save consistently
Save before spending what's left

Practical Ways to Build Your Fund

Set up automatic transfers from checking to savings
Allocate a portion of each paycheck
Use raises, bonuses, or tax refunds intentionally
Reduce one recurring expense and redirect it
Small, consistent steps create real progress.

Make It Easy With Tools

You don't have to do this manually.
Use:
Budgeting apps
Savings automation
Account aggregation tools

These tools help you track progress and stay consistent.

The Goal Is Simplicity

Your system doesn't need to be complex.
It needs to be:
Clear
Automatic
Repeatable

A Mindset Shift

An emergency fund is not "extra money."
It's not optional.
It's not something you build "one day."
It is a foundational part of financial stability.

The Second Test

A few months later, life tested her again.
Another unexpected expense.
This time?
Jane didn't panic.
She didn't open a credit card.
She didn't feel stressed.

She transferred the money from her savings account and handled it.
Simple.
Calm.
Controlled.

The Real Transformation

That moment mattered more than the dollar amount.
Because what Jane gained wasn't just savings...
It was:
Confidence

Control
Peace of mind
She wasn't just managing money anymore.
She was building security.

Closing Thought

Unexpected expenses are not a matter of if—
They are a matter of when.
The only real question is:
Will you be prepared when they happen?
Because when you have a cash reserve:
Emergencies don't become crises
Stress doesn't control your decisions
Progress doesn't stop
You stay in control.

With stability in place, you're now ready to take control of the one area that quietly holds many people back—debt.

Chapter 4 — Managing Debt & Credit: Taking Back Control

Let's start with a simple truth:
Debt is not the problem.
Unmanaged debt is.

When used intentionally, debt can be a tool.
When used carelessly, it becomes a burden.
The difference comes down to one thing:
Control.

A Question Worth Asking

Take a moment and be honest:
Do you feel in control of your debt...
Or does your debt feel like it's controlling you?

Because how you answer that question determines your next step.

Understanding Debt the Right Way

Not all debt is created equal.
Some debt can support your long-term goals:
A mortgage
Education
A business investment
Other debt tends to work against you:
High-interest credit cards
Impulse purchases
Lifestyle-driven expenses
The key is not eliminating all debt.

The key is understanding what each dollar of debt is doing in your life.

Case Study — Jane: Progress Meets Reality

By this point, Jane had made meaningful progress.
She had:
A working budget
A growing emergency fund
But there was still something lingering in the background.
Her credit cards.
Balances that built slowly over time:
A weekend here
A purchase there
That one unexpected expense
Individually, they didn't seem significant.
Together?
They told a different story.

The Hidden Cost of Debt

Debt doesn't just cost you money.
It costs you:
Flexibility
Opportunity
Peace of mind
And the most expensive part?
Interest.
Interest quietly works against you.
While investing compounds for you...
Debt compounds *against* you.

A Simple Example

A $5,000 credit card balance at high interest doesn't stay $5,000.

It grows.

Unless you actively reduce it, it keeps working in the background.

Not visibly.

But consistently.

The Emotional Side of Debt

Debt is not just math.

It's emotional.

It can create:

Stress

Avoidance

Frustration

Guilt

And when people feel overwhelmed, they often do one of two things:

Ignore it

Or make reactive decisions

Neither leads to progress.

Step One: Face It with Clarity

Before you can reduce debt...

You have to see it.

List:

Every balance

Every interest rate

Every minimum payment

No judgment.

Just clarity.

Because just like budgeting...

Awareness is where progress begins.

Case Study — Jane: Turning Point

Jane sat down one evening and listed everything out.
Three credit cards.
Balances she had been avoiding thinking about.
When she saw the total...
She felt it.
Not panic.
But clarity.
For the first time, she wasn't guessing.
She knew exactly what she was dealing with.
And that changed everything.

Step Two: Choose a Strategy

Once you know your numbers, you need a plan.
There are two common approaches:

1. The Snowball Method

Pay off the smallest balance first
Build momentum
Gain quick wins
This works because progress feels motivating.

2. The Avalanche Method

Pay off the highest interest rate first
Save more money over time
This works because it's mathematically efficient.

Which One Is Better?

The answer is simple:

The one you'll stick with.
Because consistency beats perfection.

Case Study — Jane: Choice

Jane chose the snowball method.
Not because it was mathematically perfect...
But because she needed momentum.
Her first balance was small.
She paid it off faster than expected.
That one win changed her mindset.
Now it felt possible.

Step Three: Stop Adding to the Problem

You can't make progress if debt keeps growing.
That means:
Limiting new charges
Avoiding impulse spending
Using tools like the 72-hour rule
Progress requires space.
And space comes from controlling new behavior.

The Credit Card Trap

Credit cards are not inherently bad.
But they are:
Easy
Immediate
Emotion-driven
You don't feel the impact right away.
That delay creates risk.
Because by the time the bill arrives...
The decision has already been made.

Step Four: Build a System

Debt reduction is not about motivation.
It's about systems.

Automate Your Payments

Set up:
Minimum payments
Extra principal payments
Automation removes:
Forgetting
Delays
Inconsistency

Track Your Progress

Watch balances go down.
Not obsessively—but consistently.
Because progress builds confidence.

Case Study — Jane: System

Jane automated her payments.

Every month, money flowed toward her debt—without decision fatigue.
At first, progress felt slow.
Then something happened.
Balances started dropping faster.
Not because anything changed dramatically...
But because she stayed consistent.

Step Five: Reclaim the Money

As debt decreases, something powerful happens:
Cash flow returns.

Money that was once going to interest becomes available.

That money can now:
Build savings
Fund investments
Create **freedom**

The Real Win

Paying off debt is not just about eliminating balances.
It's about creating options.
Because when your income is not tied up in payments...
You gain control.

A Common Mistake

Some people rush to invest before addressing high-interest debt.
But here's the reality:
If your debt is costing you more than your investments are earning...
You're working against yourself.
Balance matters.
Sequence matters.

A Smarter Approach

Build a starter emergency fund
Pay down high-interest debt
Continue building savings
Begin investing
Each step supports the next.

Case Study — Jane: Progress

Six months later, Jane looked at her balances again.
One card paid off
Another significantly reduced
More importantly?

She felt different.
Not overwhelmed.
Not behind.
In control.

Credit: The Other Side of the Equation

Managing debt also means understanding credit.
Your credit profile affects:
Loan approval
Interest rates
Financial opportunities

What Impacts Your Credit Score

Payment history
Amount of debt
Length of credit history
Credit mix
New credit activity
You don't need to master every detail.
But you do need to understand one key idea:
Consistency matters more than complexity.

Simple Credit Habits

Pay on time—every time
Keep balances low
Avoid unnecessary new accounts
Monitor your credit reports

Small actions... repeated consistently... create strong results.

Final Thought: Debt as a Turning Point

Debt can feel like a setback.
But it can also become a turning point.

Because once you:
Acknowledge it
Understand it
Build a plan for it
You take your power back.

Closing Thought

Debt does not define your future.
Your decisions do.
Because the goal is not just to get out of debt.

The goal is to build a financial life where debt is no longer in control.

Now that you've taken control of your debt, the next step is putting your money to work—so it begins working for you, not against you.

Chapter 5 — Retirement Planning: Building Future Income with Intention

Let's start with a powerful idea:
Time is your greatest financial advantage.
Not income.
Not investing knowledge.
Time.

Because when time and consistency work together, something remarkable happens:
Money begins to grow on itself.

The Power Most People Underestimate

Albert Einstein is often credited with calling compound interest the "eighth wonder of the world."
Why?
Because it creates a snowball effect.

You don't just earn returns on your original money.
You earn returns on your returns.
And over time, that growth accelerates.

A Simple Way to Understand It: The Rule of 72

The Rule of 72 provides a quick way to estimate how long it takes your money to double. The examples in this section are hypothetical illustrations only and are not indicative of actual investment results. Future performance cannot be guaranteed.
Just divide:

72 ÷ your rate of return
For example:
6% return → about 12 years to double
8% return → about 9 years

It's not exact—but it's powerful enough to show one key truth:

Small, consistent growth becomes meaningful over time.

Why Most People Delay Investing

Not because they don't want to.
But because:
They feel behind
They feel overwhelmed
They think they need more money to start

So they wait.

And waiting quietly becomes the most expensive decision.

Case Study — Jane: From Stability to Growth

By now, Jane had done something many people never do.
She had:
Built a budget
Created an emergency fund
Started reducing her debt
For the first time, she felt stable.
But stability wasn't the end goal.
It was the starting point.

Her First Question

Jane asked:
"Now that I'm doing better... what should I do next?"
And the answer was simple:

Start investing.

Investing Begins with a Goal

Every investment strategy should start with one thing:
Purpose.
Ask yourself:
What am I building this money for?
When will I need it?
How much will I need?
Because your answers shape:
Your timeline
Your risk level
Your strategy

Time Horizon Matters

Your time horizon is how long you have until you need the money.
Short-term (1–3 years) → lower risk
Medium-term (3–5 years) → balanced
Long-term (5+ years) → growth-focused
The longer your timeline...
The more flexibility you have to grow your money.

Risk Tolerance: Understanding Yourself

Risk tolerance isn't about numbers.
It's about *behavior.*
It answers one key question:
How will you react when your investments move up—or down?
Because markets fluctuate.
Always have.
Always will.
Your strategy must match not just your timeline...

But your ability to stay consistent.

Case Study — Jane: First Investment Decision

Jane didn't jump in all at once.
She started small.
Her employer offered a retirement plan with a match.
She learned:
If she contributed a percentage of her income...
Her employer would add more.

An employer matching contribution can *significantly* enhance retirement savings.

A Simple but Powerful Move

Jane increased her contribution just enough to get the full match.
Not because she had extra money...
But because she understood the opportunity.

And that small decision mattered more than she realized.

Why Starting Early Matters

Two people can invest the same amount.

But the one who starts earlier often ends up with *significantly* more.
Not because they invested more—
But because they gave their money more time.

The Role of Retirement Accounts

There are several common tools designed to help you build for the future.

Individual Retirement Accounts (IRAs)

Two main types:

Traditional IRA
Contributions may be tax-deductible [3]
Taxes are paid later, when withdrawn [3]

Roth IRA
Contributions are made after taxes [3]
Qualified withdrawals can be tax-free [3]

Each has advantages.
The right choice depends on your:
Income
Tax situation
Long-term goals

Employer-Sponsored Retirement Plans

Examples:
401(k)
403(b)
These plans often include:
Automatic contributions
Employer matching
Tax advantages

For many people, this is the foundation of retirement savings.

Case Study — Jane: Builds Momentum

After a few months, Jane increased her contribution again.
Just 1%.
Then another 1%.
Each increase felt small.
But over time?

Those increases added up.
And more importantly...
They became a *habit*.

A Simple Strategy: Dollar-Cost Averaging

Instead of trying to time the market, many investors use a simple approach:
Invest consistently over time.
This is called Dollar-Cost Averaging (DCA).

You invest a set amount at regular intervals—regardless of what markets are doing.

Why It Works

Removes guessing
Reduces emotional decisions
Builds consistency
It turns investing into a system—not a reaction.

Building a Portfolio: The Big Picture

A well-rounded portfolio typically includes a mix of:
Stocks (growth potential)
Bonds (stability)
Cash (liquidity)
Alternatives (in some cases)
Each plays a different role.

Asset Allocation vs. Diversification

These terms are related—but different:
Asset Allocation = how you divide your money across types of investments
Diversification = how you spread risk within those types [4]
Together, they help:
Reduce risk

Smooth out volatility
Support long-term growth

The Real Strategy

There is no "perfect" portfolio.
There is only:
An appropriate portfolio for you.
One that matches:
Your goals
Your timeline
Your comfort level

Case Study — Jane: Mindset Shift

At first, Jane thought investing was about picking the "right" investment.
Over time, she learned:
It wasn't about being perfect.
It was about being *consistent.*

What Changed for Her

Instead of asking:
"Is this the best investment?"
She started asking:
"Am I staying consistent with my plan?"
That shift changed everything.

What About Old Accounts?

As your career evolves, you may have multiple retirement accounts.
In some cases, it may make sense to:
Consolidate them
Roll them into an IRA
This can:

Simplify your financial picture
Provide more control
Align your investment strategy

A Word of Caution

Every decision has trade-offs.
Before making changes:
Consider fees
Understand tax implications
Evaluate your options carefully
When in doubt...
Work with a qualified professional.

The Bigger Picture

Retirement is not just about saving money.
It's about building future income.
Income that allows you to:
Maintain your lifestyle
Support your family
Live with independence and dignity

Case Study — Jane: Progress

One year later, Jane reviewed her progress.
She wasn't "finished."
But she was:
Investing consistently
Growing her savings
Thinking long-term

Most importantly—
She no longer felt behind.

Final Thought

You don't need to:
Time the market
Pick perfect investments
Predict the future
What you need is:
A clear goal
A simple plan
Consistent action

Closing Thought

IMPORTANT: Past performance and investment results are not guaranteed. Investment values will fluctuate and investors may experience gains or losses.

Wealth is not built in one decision.
It's built in thousands of small, intentional ones.
Because when you:
Start early
Stay consistent
Let time do its work
Your future begins to take care of itself.

This is where many people benefit from having structured guidance—not because it's complex, but because consistency matters.

As your wealth begins to grow, the next step is planning for future responsibilities—so your progress supports the life you're building.

Chapter 6 — Education Planning: Preparing for the Future with Purpose

Let's start with a simple idea:

Education is not just a cost.

It's an investment in opportunity.

Whether you're planning for your child, grandchild, or even yourself...

The goal is the same:

Prepare intentionally—so the future doesn't become a financial burden.

Why Planning Matters

Education costs continue to rise.

Without a plan:

Parents take on debt

Students graduate with financial pressure

Long-term goals get delayed

But with a plan:

You create options

You reduce stress

You stay in control

Case Study — Jane: Looking Ahead

By this point, Jane had made meaningful progress.

She had:

Built an emergency fund

Reduced her debt

Started investing
For the first time, she wasn't focused on catching up.
She was thinking ahead.

A New Question

Jane asked:
"How do I prepare for future milestones... without losing the progress I've made?"
That's the shift.
Not reacting to life...
Planning for it.

Where Do You Start?

Start with clarity.
Ask yourself:
Who is this for?
When will the money be needed?
How much might it cost?
You don't need perfect answers.
You need *direction.*

Understanding 529 Plans

One of the most common tools for education planning is the 529 plan.

It is designed specifically to help families save for education expenses.

How It Works

You contribute after-tax money into an account.
That money:
Grows tax-deferred

Can be withdrawn tax-free for qualified education expenses

What Counts as Qualified Expenses?

Tuition
Fees
Books
Computers and equipment
In some cases: room and board
529 plans can also be used for:
Certain certifications
Apprenticeship programs
K–12 tuition (within limits)

Who Can Contribute?

One of the advantages of a 529 plan is flexibility.
Anyone can contribute:
Parents
Grandparents
Family members
Even friends
This creates opportunities for collaborative planning.

Case Study — Jane: Approach

Jane didn't have children yet.
But she understood the value of starting early.
Instead of waiting, she made a simple decision:

She opened a 529 plan with a small monthly contribution.
Not because she needed it immediately—
But because she knew what time could do.

Tax Considerations

529 contributions are considered gifts for tax purposes.
There are annual limits, but in most cases:

You can contribute regularly without triggering gift taxes.

Some states also offer tax deductions or credits for contributions.

A Key Principle

The biggest advantage of education planning is not complexity.
It's consistency over time.

Financial Aid: What to Know

At some point, most families will interact with financial aid.
And the starting point is FAFSA:
Free Application for Federal Student Aid

What FAFSA Does

It evaluates:
Family income
Assets
Financial situation
Then determines potential eligibility for:
Grants
Loans
Work-study programs [5]

A Common Misconception

Many people assume:
"If I earn too much, I won't qualify."
That's not always true.
Financial aid decisions consider multiple factors.
Which is why the best approach is simple:
Apply—regardless of assumptions.

How Assets Are Considered

Different assets are treated differently in financial aid calculations.
For example:
Some savings accounts count directly
Some education-specific accounts are treated more favorably

Understanding this helps you plan more effectively.

Avoiding Common Mistakes

Here are a few simple ways to stay on track:
Submit FAFSA early
Renew it each year [6]
Understand deadlines
Keep documentation organized

Small oversights can lead to missed opportunities.

Case Study — Jane: Mindset Shift

Jane realized something important:
Education planning wasn't about predicting everything.
It was about preparing enough.

Her Strategy

She focused on three things:
Consistent contributions
Understanding her options
Staying flexible
She didn't try to solve every future scenario.
She built a system that could adapt.

Balancing Priorities

One important rule:

Don't sacrifice your financial foundation for education savings.

That means:

Maintain your emergency fund

Continue retirement contributions

Avoid taking on unnecessary debt

Because while education is important...

So is your long-term financial stability.

Other Tools and Considerations

In addition to 529 plans, families may consider:

Tax credits (education-related)

Student loan interest deductions

Scholarship opportunities

Each plays a role—but none replaces proper planning.

The Bigger Picture

Education planning is not just about money.

It's about:

Opportunity

Flexibility

Freedom of choice

Because when financial pressure is reduced...

Decisions become clearer.

Case Study — Jane: Progress

Over time, Jane's account slowly grew.

It wasn't dramatic.

But it was consistent.

And consistency builds confidence.

She no longer saw future milestones as financial threats.

She saw them as planned opportunities.

Final Thought

You don't need to:
Predict the exact cost
Save everything at once
Have a perfect plan
You need to:
Start early
Stay consistent
Adjust along the way
Planning for education is not about certainty.
It's about preparation.
Because when you prepare:
You reduce stress
You create opportunity
You give yourself—and others—options

And options are one of the greatest forms of financial freedom.

With a plan for the future in place, the next step is protecting everything you've built—so your progress lasts.

Chapter 7 — Protecting Assets & Managing Risk: Securing What You've Built

By this point, you've done something powerful.
You've:
Built awareness
Created a plan
Developed better habits
Started saving and investing
Now comes the next step:
Protecting what you've built.
Because building wealth is only half the equation.
Keeping it—and protecting it—is the other half.

Why Protection Matters

Life is unpredictable.
Not if—but *when*—something unexpected happens:
Illness
Injury
Job interruption
Loss
Without protection:
Assets can disappear
Plans can unravel
Progress can reverse
With protection:
You stay on track—even when life happens.

Case Study — Jane: Next Realization

By now, Jane had built momentum.
She had:
Paid down debt
Built savings
Started investing

But during one of her financial check-ins, she realized something:
"I've spent all this time building... but what protects it?"
It was a new kind of question.
Less about growth...
More about protection.

Risk Is Part of the Equation

Every financial plan has risk.
The goal is not to eliminate it.
The goal is to manage it intelligently.
And that's where protection tools come in.

The Role of Insurance

Insurance is not exciting.
It doesn't feel like progress.
But it plays a critical role.

It protects your future from being derailed by the unexpected.

A Simple Truth About Insurance

Years ago, I heard someone say: "People typically buy insurance for one of two reasons:
They love someone
They owe someone"

Either way, it's about responsibility.

Life Insurance: Protecting the People Who Depend on You

Life insurance provides financial protection to those you leave behind.
It helps ensure that:
Your family isn't financially burdened
Your goals continue, even if you're not there

Two Primary Types

Term Life Insurance

Covers a specific time period
Typically more affordable
No cash value

Permanent Life Insurance

Covers your entire life
May build cash value
Higher cost, more complexity

What Determines Your Need?

When evaluating life insurance, consider:
Income replacement
Debt obligations
Family needs
Long-term goals
There's no one-size-fits-all answer.
The right coverage depends on your situation.

Case Study — Jane: Perspective

Jane didn't initially think she needed life insurance.

But after reviewing her finances, she realized:
If something happened to her...
Her obligations wouldn't disappear
Her family might be impacted
So she explored a simple term policy.
Not overcomplicated.
Just appropriate.

Disability Income Insurance: Protecting Your Ability to Earn

This may be one of the most overlooked protections.
Your income is likely your greatest financial asset.
Without it:
Bills don't stop
Expenses continue
Goals get delayed

Disability income insurance replaces a portion of your income if you can't work due to illness or injury.

Key Considerations

When evaluating a policy, look at:
Benefit amount (how much income is replaced)
Elimination period (how long before payments begin)
Benefit duration (how long payments last)

Definition of disability (what qualifies as being unable to work)

Case Study — Jane: Insight

Jane had always assumed:
"I'm healthy—I don't need this."
But then she realized:

Disability insurance isn't about what's likely.
It's about what's possible.

That shift changed her thinking.

Long-Term Care: Planning for Extended Needs

As we live longer, the likelihood of needing long-term care increases.
This includes:
In-home care
Assisted living
Nursing facilities
These costs can be significant—and often are not fully covered by traditional health insurance.

Options to Consider

Traditional long-term care policies
Life insurance with long-term care riders
Hybrid solutions
Each option comes with trade-offs.
The key is understanding what fits your situation.

The Real Risk

The biggest risk is not planning for care.
Because without a plan:
Savings can be depleted
Family members may carry the burden
Financial independence can be compromised

Annuities: Creating Income Stability

Some individuals use annuities to:
Generate retirement income
Provide protection
Add predictability
There are several types, including:
Fixed

Variable
Indexed
Immediate
Each has different features, risks, and costs.

A Balanced View

Annuities can be useful in the right situation. They may involve fees, surrender charges, limited liquidity, insurance-company claims-paying risk, inflation risk, and opportunity costs. Variable annuities are subject to market risk, including possible loss of principal.
But they are not necessary for everyone.
As with any financial tool:
Fit matters more than features.

Case Study — Jane: Approach to Protection

Jane didn't try to solve everything at once.
She focused on:
Understanding her risks
Prioritizing what mattered
Taking simple, thoughtful action
She didn't aim for perfection.
She aimed for progress and protection.

Estate Planning: More Than Just Assets

Estate planning is often misunderstood.
It's not just about distributing money.
It's about:
Protecting your wishes
Providing clarity
Reducing confusion for loved ones

Key Components of an Estate Plan

1. Beneficiary Designations
Keep them updated—especially after major life events.
These often override what's written in a will.

2. A Will
Outlines how your assets should be distributed.
Allows you to:
Name an executor
Appoint guardians

3. Powers of Attorney
Allows someone to act on your behalf if needed.
Includes:
Financial decisions
Healthcare decisions

4. Living Will / Advanced Directive
Documents your medical preferences
Provides clarity in difficult situations

Why This Matters

Without a plan:
Decisions may be delayed
Conflicts may arise
Outcomes may not reflect your intentions
With a plan:
Clarity replaces confusion.

Case Study — Jane: Final Step in This Phase

At this point in her journey, Jane realized something powerful:
She wasn't just managing money anymore.

She was building a system.
A system that:
Creates growth
Supports stability
Protects progress

The Big Picture

Every financial decision comes back to three things:
Building
Growing
Protecting
Neglect one—and the others become vulnerable.

Final Thought

You don't need:
Complex strategies
Perfect knowledge
Every solution at once
You need:
Awareness
Intentional decisions
Consistent action

Closing Thought

Life will always carry uncertainty.
But uncertainty doesn't have to create instability.
Because when you protect what you've built:

You give your future the strength to withstand the unexpected.

Now that your financial foundation is built, growing, and protected… it's time to bring everything together and turn it into lasting transformation.

Chapter 8 — Take Action: Your Financial Transformation Starts Now

The Moment Everything Changes

You've made it here.
And that matters.

Because most people never take the time to truly understand how their financial life works—let alone take steps to change it.

But you did.
You've explored:

How mindset shapes your decisions
How habits create outcomes
How budgeting brings clarity
How saving builds stability
How investing creates growth
How protection preserves what you've built

You now understand something many people never fully grasp:

Money is not just math.
It's behavior.
It's mindset.
It's systems.

But Here's the Truth

Knowledge alone does not create change.

Action does.

Consistent action.

Intentional action.

Your action.

Transformation doesn't happen overnight.

It doesn't come from one big decision.

It comes from a series of small, repeatable choices—made day after day.

You Are Standing at a Crossroads

Right now, you have a choice:

You can:

Close this book

Feel motivated for a few days

Then slowly fall back into old patterns

Or...

You can decide that this moment means something more.

That this is not just information—

It's a turning point.

Case Study — Jane: Transformation

Let's come back to Jane.

When you first met her, she:

Felt behind

Made reactive decisions

Lived without clarity

She wasn't irresponsible.

She was unaware.

Step by Step, She Changed

She:
Questioned her habits
Built a realistic budget
Created an emergency fund
Took control of her debt
Began investing
Protected what she built
Nothing she did was perfect.
But everything she did was ***intentional***.

And That Changed Everything

Jane didn't become wealthy overnight.
But she became something far more important:
She became in ***control***.
She no longer:
Compared her life to others
Reacted emotionally to money
Felt constantly behind

She built something steady.
Something sustainable.
Something real.

Now It's Your Turn – to Keep up with You

Jane's story is not unique.
It's possible for anyone willing to make a decision:
To become *intentional*.

Step One: Revisit Your Vision

Before anything else, ask yourself:
What do I want my financial life to feel like?
What do I want to protect?

What do I want my money to help me experience?

Not just numbers.
Clarity.
Purpose.
Confidence.

Because Without Vision...

Financial planning becomes mechanical.
With vision, it becomes ***meaningful***.

Step Two: Build Your System

Every financially successful person has one thing in common:
They have a system.
Not just good intentions.
Not just discipline.
A *system*.
Your System Includes:
Automatic Saving
Consistency beats intensity.
A Living Budget
Flexible. Realistic. Aligned with your life.
A Debt Strategy
Clear. Focused. Trackable.
An Investment Plan
Simple. Consistent. Long-term.

Why This Matters

Because systems remove guesswork.
They remove emotion.
They create progress—even when you're not thinking about it.

Step Three: Strengthen Your Habits

Everything comes back to behavior.
Start with simple habits:
The 72-hour rule
Monthly money check-ins
Tracking progress
Automating decisions
These small actions compound—just like money does.

Step Four: Remove What Holds You Back

Most setbacks come from three things:
1. Not Knowing Where to Start
Start with awareness. Track your spending.

2. Feeling Overwhelmed
Break progress into small steps.
Not everything today.
Something today.

3. Believing It Takes Too Long
Time will pass either way.
The question is:
Will you move forward with it?

Your 90-Day Transformation Plan

Here's a simple roadmap to begin:

Days 1–7

Define your vision
List your goals
Track your spending

Days 8–30

Build a working budget
Start a small emergency fund
Automate one financial action

Month 2

Increase savings contributions
Reduce one recurring expense
Pay down specific debt

Month 3

Review your progress
Adjust your plan
Strengthen your system

After 90 Days

Your life won't be perfect.
But it will be different.
More clear.
More controlled.
More intentional.

You Don't Need to Be Perfect

Every person who has created financial stability started in the same place:
Uncertain
Overwhelmed
Learning

They started anyway.

A New Identity

This is not just about what you do.

It's about who you *become*.

You Are Becoming Someone Who:

Makes intentional decisions

Values clarity over comparison

Chooses discipline over impulse

Builds progress over time

The Truth About Wealth

Wealth is not:

What people see

What you post

What others think

Wealth is:

Control

Stability

Freedom

Peace

Final Reflection

Take a moment and think about this:

If you continue making small, intentional changes...

Where will you be in:

One year?

Five years?

Ten years?

Because the future you want is not built later.

It's built **now**.

Final Words

You don't need to keep up with anyone else.

You don't need to prove anything.

You don't need to chase an image.

You only need to do one thing:

Keep up with **YOU**!

Read this slowly:
"I am someone who makes intentional financial decisions.
I build with purpose.
I act with clarity.
I stay consistent.
I choose progress over perfection.
I am building a life that aligns with who I truly am."
Because this is not the end of your journey.
This is the beginning.
And the decisions you make from this point forward...
Will define everything that comes next.

Next Step: If You Want Guidance

If this book helped you think differently about money... imagine what happens when you apply it with a personalized plan.
I work with individuals and families who are ready to:
Take control of their finances
Build long-term wealth
Create a clear, structured financial strategy
If that sounds like you, visit the website below:
www.vincentcperry.com/

References

[1] Board of Governors of the Federal Reserve System. (2025). Report on the Economic Well-Being of U.S. Households in 2024 (Survey of Household Economics and Decision-making). Available at: https://www.federalreserve.gov/publications/2025-economic-well-being-of-us-households-in-2024-savings-and-investments.htm

[2] Bankrate. (2026, February 4). Bankrate's 2026 Annual Emergency Savings Report. Available at: https://www.bankrate.com/banking/savings/emergency-savings-report/

[3] Internal Revenue Service (IRS). (2025). Traditional and Roth IRAs. Available at: https://www.irs.gov/retirement-plans/traditional-and-roth-iras

[4] U.S. Securities and Exchange Commission (SEC), Investor.gov. (n.d.). Asset Allocation and Diversification. Available at: https://www.investor.gov/introduction-investing/getting-started/asset-allocation

[5] U.S. Department of Education. (n.d.). The FAFSA®: What You Need to Know. Available at: https://www.ed.gov/higher-education/paying-college/fafsar-what-you-need-know

[6] Federal Student Aid (studentaid.gov). (n.d.). FAFSA® Application Overview. Available at: https://studentaid.gov/h/apply-for-aid/fafsa

About the Author

Vincent C. Perry, CFP® is an author, speaker, and educator with three decades of experience helping individuals and families build clarity, confidence, and long-term financial stability through personalized advice. www.VincentCPerry.com

www.ingramcontent.com/pod-product-compliance
Lightning Source LLC
LaVergne TN
LVHW100733061126
851857LV00011B/518

* 9 7 9 8 2 3 4 1 8 2 5 4 8 *